I0142227

The Jokez R On U

Leslie Guity

BK

ROYSTON
Publishing

BK Royston Publishing LLC

P. O. Box 4321

Jeffersonville, IN 47131

http://www.bkroystonpublishing.com

bkroystonpublishing@gmail.com

Copyright 2021

Cover by: Anissa Moore

ISBN: 978-1-955063-16-6

Printed in the USA

Dedication

The creation of The Jokez R on U was motivated by all the giggles, sighs, eye-rolling, and groaning I received over the years from family, friends, and even strangers I met EVERYWHERE. They are the ones who demanded moments of their life back after I relentlessly subjected them to all the head-scratching jokes and silly riddles I just had to release from my own head.

This book is dedicated to you!

THANK YOU, THANK YOU, THANK YOU!

You are ALL awesome!

Preface

I have been told that my brain sees, thinks, and experiences life from a "different" perspective, shall I say, that is not the norm. Were you told the same? If so, THEN YOU ARE FABULOUS TOO!

My brother, Ruben, told me that they ("THEY" could mean scientists—perhaps) need to create a roller-coaster tour through my brain. Apparently, because I don't think like everybody else thinks. My brain is constantly in creative mode, so you never know what you might see on THAT tour.

Question: Are you an "in-the-box" thinker, or do you think outside of the box? I guarantee that my jokes will cause you to think outside of the box. You have no choice but to!

The selection of seventy-seven jokes and riddles is created for your laughing pleasure. I hope this book brings a smile to your day and joy to your heart, especially during trying times. It is always necessary to laugh to heal the soul.

At the end of this book, you will be given a fun and challenging assignment. Enjoy!

So, are you ready to laugh? Get ready to hold your stomach and let the laughing begin.

LET'S GO!

1 What do you call a smiling woman with blue lipstick on?

Blue cheese

2 What do a little girl and a bag carrier have in common?

A dolly

3 What political position does a horse run for?

Mare

4 What kind of scary animal do you only see at night?

Nightmare

5 The singing stallion usually sings all day and night. One day, he was not singing, and was asked why he was not singing.

He replied, while holding his throat, "I'm horse!"

6 The butter knife complimented the steak knife.

It said, "You look sharp!"

7 Mr. Cocoa was screaming for help because he was being mugged!

8 "The client wanted a mugshot so the photographer took a picture of a coffee cup."

9 Mr. Homes got sick...he caught cabin fever.

10 The sink asked the toilet, "Are you alright?"

"You look flushed."

11 When Egbert is trying to be serious, it's all yokes aside.

Ha! Ha! Ha!

12 The eggs were teasing each other.

"Can't you take a yoke?"

13 Eggs think humans are comedians because they have them cracking up!

14 What type of boat can people play basketball on?

A courtship

15 A lady threatened to sue the spa owner because the staff kept trying to put a diaper on her.

The owner responded, "You said you wanted to be pampered."

16 The dirty man must have loved the bathtub because he put a ring on it.

17 The park ranger told the animals not to bother the humans. A visitor went to the Service Center all scratched up. The park ranger found the bear and asked, "What did you do?"

The bear said, "What? I bearly touched him."

18 Lil bear did not like to wear shoes; he liked being bearfooted.

19 What do you call a person singing high notes in the bubble bath?

Soap opera

20 What do you call a pizza that is leaning over to the side?

Tower of Pizza
(Tower of Pisa)

21

My guy friend has a girlfriend, and loves her so much. She even finishes his sentences.

Her name is Dot.

22

My friend cannot spend the night at my house anymore because she wakes up too early.

Her name is Dawn.

23

Who do you always have to call to your table before you eat?

Grace

24

What do you call a pig bathing in the sun?

Bacon

25 What do you call a single strand of hair growing on someone's back?

A backlash

26 How do we know a bird can tell time?

He has a birdwatch.

27 My friend agreed to be my maid of honor, so I gave her a vacuum cleaner and a crown!

28 I had a boyfriend, but I quit him because he lies. I saw right through him. He was the ex-Ray.

29 Had another boy-friend who kept ask-ing me to say, "Aaah." I thought he was weird...his name was Arthur Dontas.

30 Arthur has a brother who is also interested in the inside of people's mouths. His name is Perry O. Dontas.

31 A guy went to the dentist because his anatomy class told him his body has a cavity!

32 My friend helps fix flat tires. His name is Jack.

33 My friend is such a pushover everyone walks on top of him. His name is Matt.

34 I had a boyfriend who used to steal from me. His name was Rob.

35 My friend really looked good with a suit. His name is Ty.

36 What do you call the people who make sandwiches at the deli?

Subcontractors

37

What kind of bird
tells
mediocre jokes?

Cornish hen

38

What do you call a
bird that is strong
enough to lift a car?

A crane

39 What kind of seafood do you eat to make you stronger?

Mussels

40 What catholic church do dogs go to?

Saint Bernard

41

What animal is always cold?

A chili dog

42

What is another name for a yellow cow?

Corned beef

43

What do you get when cows dance?

Milkshakes

44

What do you get when a cow dances after eating strawberries?

Strawberry shake

45

A nine-month preg-
nant lady was trying
to finish all her
errands before her
baby came. She went
into labor at the post
office. An ambulance
was called, but they
hadn't arrived yet, so
the postman
delivered the baby.
The postman handed
the baby to the lady
and said, "You got
male."

46

What kind of lotion
did Ms. Piglet use?

Lard
.

47 What kind of car does a snowman drive?

A snowmobile

48 DJ Santa yelled, "Everybody in the house say, Ho, Ho, Ho!"

49

There was a cow counseling all the other cows on the farm. What do you call the advice the cow was giving?

Steak tips

50

What article of clothing smells horrible?

A windbreaker

51

What other body part can you talk out of besides your mouth?

Your but-tocks

52

What is the name of the band that has people bouncing?

Rubber band

53 A lady came in for her first day of work. When they showed the lady her desk, she screamed. They asked what's wrong, and she said, "There's a mouse next to the computer."

54 One of our relatives got married and had a great reception. She is our Ant-Enna!

55 I have another relative who always snaps at people. His name is Curt.

56 And his brother is always bothering people. His name is Nat.

57

How does a horse greet you?

Hay (Hey)

58

Where does Ms. Pony shop for food?

Haymarket. (*This is a Boston joke.*)

59 Mr. Melon and his fiancé had to plan their wedding because they cantaloupe!

60 Mr. Orange can blast music because he got the juice!

61 Mr. Navel was flirting with the oranges in the bag. His girlfriend was mad. He said, "Don't worry baby, you're my main squeeze!"

62 Why is everyone drunk at night?

Moonshine

63

In what bank can you launder money?

Riverbank

64

Eagles take aspirin because they soar!

65 Someone told me they had surgery and now only have half of a colon. I said, "Oh, so you have a semi-colon?"

66 The fabric thinks the sewing machine is funny because it keeps it in stitches.

67 Mr. Belt was at the bar...waisted.

68 What is another name for a rude bird?

Jerk chicken

69

The chicken was in a play and didn't really know his lines—he was just winging it.

70

Name a bird with an attitude.

Sweet and sour chicken

71

What do you call a bird with a bad tan?

Crispy chicken

72

In basketball, what position does a chicken play?

Wing

73

What movie does the President star in?

Casa Blanca

74

All the ducks were hanging out in the pond. One told a joke, and they all started quacking up.

75

What type of music do rodents hate to hear?

Trap music

76

The astronaut wanted to make fried rice, so they used a moon wok.

What do you call a person who is money crazy?

A dough nut

Ha, Ha, The Jokez R on U.
After you have finished laughing, here's your assignment:
Use the words below to create
three jokes of your own (one
joke per word).

Nutcase
Scramble
Car

Then share your jokes with
friends and family to see if you,
too, can tickle people's funny
bones. You can do It! Spread
the love and laughter!

1. _____
   _____
   _____
   _____
   _____
   _____

2 _____
   _____
   _____
   _____
   _____
   _____

3. _____
   _____
   _____
   _____
   _____
   _____

Bio

Leslie Guity is a Boston native and a first-generation Honduran American.

She is a vocalist and vocal instructor whose versatility includes acting, choreography, theatre production, and modeling.

Leslie is also a published author of, "Music is the Key" and "I'm 25." She is also an aspiring songwriter, poet, and jokester. Last but not least, she is a mom of five beautiful children, and a grandmother of five. She endeavors to shine her light with her God-given gifts.

www.ingramcontent.com/pod-product-compliance
Lightning Source LLC
LaVergne TN
LVHW010023070426
835508LV00001B/29